W9-CUT-961

GOLDILOCKS and the 3 BEARS

Book Design & Production: Slangman Kids (a division of Slangman Inc. and Slangman Publishing)

Copy Editor: Julie Bobrick
Illustrated by: "Migs!" Sandoval
Translators: Teut Deese & Petra Wirth
Proofreader: Kai Cofer

Published by: Slangman Kids (a division of Slangman Inc. and Slangman Publishing) 12206 Hillslope Street, Studio City, CA 91604 •USA • Toll Free Telephone from USA: 1-877-SLANGMAN (1-877-752-6462) • From outside the USA: 1-818-SLANGMAN (1-818-752-6462) • Worldwide Fax 1-413-647-1589 • Email: info@slangman.com • Website: www.slangman.com

"Migs!" Sandoval ✷ our illustrator ✷

Miguel *"Migs!"* Sandoval has been drawing cartoons since the age of 6 and has worked on numerous national commercials and movies as a sculptor, model builder, and illustrator. He was born in Los Angeles and was raised in a bilingual household, speaking English and Spanish. He currently lives in San Francisco where he is working on his new comic book series!

ISBN10: 1891888-838
ISBN13: 978189888-830
Printed in the U.S.A.

10 9 8 7 6 5 4 3 2 1

Order Form

Preview chapters & shop online!
www.slangman.com

SHIP TO: _____

_____

_____

_____

Contact/Phone/Email: _____

SHIPPING

Domestic Orders

SURFACE MAIL
(Delivery time 5-7 business days).
Add $5 shipping/handling for the first item, $1.50 for each additional item.

RUSH SERVICE
Available at extra charge. Contact us for details.

International Orders

SURFACE MAIL
(Delivery time 6-8 weeks).
Add $6 shipping/handling for the first item, $2 for each additional item. Note that shipping to some countries may be more expensive. Contact us for details.

AIRMAIL (approx. 3-5 business days)
Available at extra charge. Contact us for details.

Method of Payment (Check one):

☐ Personal Check or Money Order
(Must be in U.S. funds and drawn on a U.S. bank.)

☐ VISA   ☐ Master Card   ☐ Discover   ☐ American Express   ☐ JCB

Credit Card Number

Signature   Expiration Date

QTY	ISBN-13	TITLE	PRICE	LEVEL	TOTAL COST
		English to CHINESE (Mandarin)			
	9781891888-793	**Cinderella**	$14.95	1	
	9781891888-854	**Goldilocks**	$14.95	2	
	9781891888-915	**Beauty and the Beast**	$14.95	3	
		English to FRENCH			
	9781891888-755	**Cinderella**	$14.95	1	
	9781891888-816	**Goldilocks**	$14.95	2	
	9781891888-878	**Beauty and the Beast**	$14.95	3	
		English to GERMAN			
	9781891888-762	**Cinderella**	$14.95	1	
	9781891888-830	**Goldilocks**	$14.95	2	
	9781891888-885	**Beauty and the Beast**	$14.95	3	
		English to HEBREW			
	9781891888-922	**Cinderella**	$14.95	1	
	9781891888-939	**Goldilocks**	$14.95	2	
	9781891888-946	**Beauty and the Beast**	$14.95	3	
		English to ITALIAN			
	9781891888-779	**Cinderella**	$14.95	1	
	9781891888-823	**Goldilocks**	$14.95	2	
	9781891888-892	**Beauty and the Beast**	$14.95	3	
		English to JAPANESE			
	9781891888-786	**Cinderella**	$14.95	1	
	9781891888-847	**Goldilocks**	$14.95	2	
	9781891888-908	**Beauty and the Beast**	$14.95	3	
		English to SPANISH			
	9781891888-748	**Cinderella**	$14.95	1	
	9781891888-809	**Goldilocks**	$14.95	2	
	9781891888-861	**Beauty and the Beast**	$14.95	3	
		Japanese to ENGLISH 絵本で えいご を学ぼう			
	9781891888-038	**Cinderella**	$14.95	1	
	9781891888-045	**Goldilocks**	$14.95	2	
	9781891888-052	**Beauty and the Beast**	$14.95	3	
		Korean to ENGLISH 동화를 통한 ENGLISH 배우기			
	9781891888-076	**Cinderella**	$14.95	1	
	9781891888-106	**Goldilocks**	$14.95	2	
	9781891888-113	**Beauty and the Beast**	$14.95	3	
		Spanish to ENGLISH Aprende INGLÉS con cuentos de hadas			
	9781891888-953	**Cinderella**	$14.95	1	
	9781891888-960	**Goldilocks**	$14.95	2	
	9781891888-977	**Beauty and the Beast**	$14.95	3	

Total for Merchandise

Sales Tax *(California residents only add applicable sales tax)*

Shipping *(See left)*

ORDER GRAND TOTAL

Prices subject to change

SLANGMAN® KIDS
(a division of Slangman Publishing)

** TO PLACE AN ORDER - CALL, FAX, OR EMAIL: **
Phone: 1-818-752-6462 • Fax: 1-413-647-1589
Email: info@slangman.com • Web: www.slangman.com
12206 Hillslope Street • Studio City, CA 91604

(FORM 071606)

Dedication

The entire "Foreign Language Through Fairy Tales" series is dedicated to all the children of the world.

It is through their understanding, appreciation, and celebration of our differences that the world will become a better and safer place for us all.

A few things to remember...

- In this fairy tale, you'll notice that some of the German words have a new letter of the alphabet. It's the letter "ß" which looks a lot like our letter "B," but it's not! It's called an "eszett" which is used to represent "ss." For example:

  foot = **Fuss**, but it's always written as **Fuß**.
  big = **gross**, but it's always written as **groß**.

- You'll notice that in German, all nouns (those words that represent a person, place, or thing) begin with an uppercase letter. That's because in German, ALL nouns are written this way! For example:

  girl=**Mädchen** • house=**Haus** • party=**Fest** • prince=**Prinz**

- The words in *green italics* throughout this fairy tale are words you've already learned in the previous level! Do you still remember what they mean?

1

Bär

Papa

Mama

Once upon a time, there was a [bear] family.

The **Bär** family lived in a **Haus** in the forest.

There was a [papa] **Bär** who was very **groß**,

a [mama] **Bär** who was very **hübsch**, and a

baby bear who was very little. The **Babybär**, who was very **klein**, was also extremely *stattlich* like his **Papa**. The **Papa Bär** was very much *verliebt* with the **Mama Bär**

Babybär

klein

3

Spaziergang ◀ and they were indeed proud of their **Bär** family. One day, the **Mama Bär** prepared some soup for lunch, but it was too hot. While it cooled off, the **Bär** family went for a stroll.

Meanwhile in a town nearby, there lived a *Mädchen*, who was very **klein**, named Goldilocks. She was very *traurig* because she never had anything fun to do.

5

She thought for a **Moment** and decided to take a **Spaziergang** in the forest. Very soon, she came upon a **Haus**

Tür ← and knocked on the door but no one

was there. So she opened the **Tür**, put
one **Fuß** inside the **Haus**, and said
"Hello? Is anyone home?" She was
very tired after her long **Spaziergang**

müde

7

and since no one answered, she walked inside the **Haus**. She looked around and was very **glücklich** to see a (table) in the (kitchen) with food on it!

Tisch ←

Küche ←

8

She quickly approached the **Tisch** in the **Küche** and was super extra *glücklich* because there on the **Tisch** in the **Küche** was a [bowl] —

→ **Schüssel**

9

eins
zwei
drei

but not just one **Schüssel**. There were one, two, three of them! **Eins**, **zwei**, **drei** sitting on the **Tisch** in the **Küche**. She took a taste from the **Schüssel** that belonged to the

Papa Bär and said, "This is too hot!"

→ **heiß**

Then she took a taste from the **Schüssel**

that belonged to the **Mama Bär** and said,

"This is too cold!" Then she took a taste from

→ **kalt**

the **Schüssel** of the **Babybär** and said,
"Ahhh. This one isn't too **heiß**. It isn't too
kalt. It's just right!" The **Schüssel** was very
klein and she ate everything in it. *"Danke!"*

she said to the empty **Schüssel**. Well, now she was even more **müde** than ever after eating so much. So, she decided to rest. In the living room, she saw an (armchair)... but not just

Sessel

one **Sessel**. There were **eins**, **zwei**, **drei** of them! **Eins, zwei, drei**! So, she sat down in the **Sessel** of the **Papa Bär** and said, "Oh! This **Sessel** is too [hard]!"

hart ←

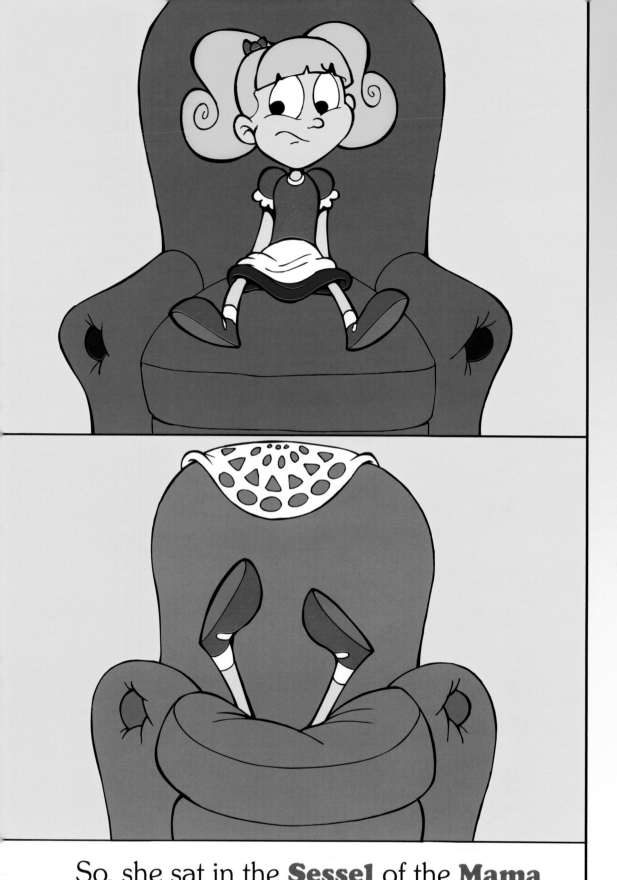

So, she sat in the **Sessel** of the **Mama Bär** and said, "Oh! This **Sessel** is too ⌊soft⌋!" Then she sat in the **Sessel** of the **Babybär** and said,

→ weich

"Ahhh. This **Sessel** isn't too **hart**. It isn't too **weich**. It's just right!" But just as she got comfortable... *Crack!* The **Sessel** broke and completely fell apart!

Still **müde**, she decided to look for the bedroom to take a nap. In front of her, she saw a [bed]… but not just one **Bett**. There were **eins**, **zwei**, **drei** of them!

Bett

Eins, **zwei**, **drei**! So, she tried the **Bett** of the **Papa Bär**, but it was too **hart**. Then she tried the **Bett** of the **Mama Bär**, but it was too **weich**. Finally, she tried the

Bett of the **Babybär** and said, "Ahhh. This **Bett** isn't too **hart**. It isn't too **weich**. It's just right!" And she fell asleep. At that **Moment**, the **Bär** family returned from their **Spaziergang**. As soon as they walked in, the **Papa Bär** noticed something strange. "Someone's been eating my soup!"

said the **Papa Bär**. "And someone's been eating my soup!" said the **Mama Bär**. "And someone's been eating MY soup and ate it all up!" cried the **Babybär**.

21

"Look!" said the **Papa Bär**. "Someone's been sitting in my **Sessel**!" "And someone's been sitting in my **Sessel**, as well!" said the **Mama Bär**.

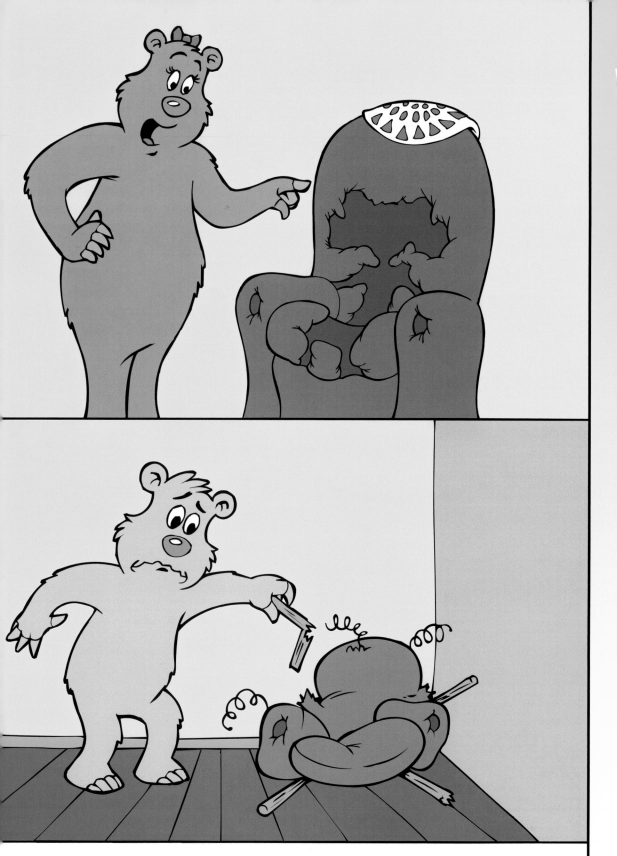

"And someone's been sitting in my **Sessel** and broke it into pieces!" cried the **Babybär**. Suddenly, the **Papa Bär**, the **Mama Bär**, and the

Babybär heard snoring coming from the bedroom, so they went in to look. "Someone's been sleeping in my **Bett**!" said the **Papa Bär**. "And

someone's been sleeping in my **Bett**,
as well" said the **Mama Bär**. "And
someone's been sleeping in my **Bett**
and there she is!" shouted the **Babybär**.

Just then, Goldilocks woke up and was
surprised to see the **Bär** family! The
Bär family thought the **Mädchen**
was very *böse* to use their *Haus*

without permission! So, Goldilocks said to the **Papa Bär**, "Oh, *danke* for letting me eat food from your **Schüssel**, sit in your **Sessel**, and lie in your **Bett**!" Goldiocks

said "*Danke!*" again expecting the **Bär** family to say, "*Gern geschehen!*" but they were angry that she caused so much trouble in their *Haus* and the **Bär** family growled

at her. So, she slowly stood up on the **Bett**
of the **Babybär**, and nervously said,
"Well, *Danke* for having me and... *auf*
Wiedersehen!" And with that, Goldilocks

jumped off the **Bett**, and dashed out the front **Tür**, running as fast as each *Fuß* could move. Needless to say, she never returned to visit the *Haus* of the **Bär** family again.